A Taste of culture

Foods of England

Barbara Sheen

KIDHAVEN PRESS
A part of Gale, Cengage Learning

GALE
CENGAGE Learning™

Detroit • New York • San Francisco • New Haven, Conn • Waterville, Maine • London

LIBRARY OF CONGRESS CATALOGING-IN-PUBLICATION DATA

Sheen, Barbara.
　Foods of England / by Barbara Sheen.
　　p. cm. -- (A taste of culture)
　Includes bibliographical references and index.
　ISBN 978-0-7377-5881-8 (hardcover)
　1. Cooking, English--Juvenile literature. 2. Food habits--England--Juvenile literature. 3. England--Social life and customs--Juvenile literature. I. Title. II. Series.
　TX717.S472 2011
　394.1'20942--dc22

2011006944

Kidhaven Press
27500 Drake Rd.
Farmington Hills MI 48331

ISBN-13: 978-0-7377-5881-8
ISBN-10: 0-7377-5881-3

Printed in the United States of America
1 2 3 4 5 6 7 15 14 13 12 11

Printed by Bang Printing, Brainerd, MN, 1st Ptg., 05/2011

Contents

Chapter 1
A Fertile Land   4

Chapter 2
Simple and Delicious   17

Chapter 3
It Is Time for Tea   29

Chapter 4
Happy Holidays   41

Metric Conversions   52

Notes   53

Glossary   55

For Further Exploration   57

Index   59

Picture Credits   63

About the Author   64

A Fertile Land

England is a European country located on the southern part of the island of Great Britain. It is separated from the European continent by the English Channel. It is an independent country whose government is united with three other countries—Wales, Scotland, and Northern Ireland—forming a political body known as the United Kingdom of Great Britain and Northern Ireland, or the UK.

England has long coastlines, many inland waterways, rolling grasslands, rich soil, and a mild, rainy climate—all of which makes it an excellent place to catch fish, and raise crops and livestock. English cooks have lots of ingredients to work with. Meat, fish and seafood,

Shetland Islands

Atlantic Ocean

Orkney Islands

FOOD REGIONS OF ENGLAND

SCOTLAND

North Sea

Glasgow
★

UNITED KINGDOM

NORTHERN IRELAND

Belfast ★

Dublin ★

IRELAND

ENGLAND

WALES

Cardiff ★

Thames

★
London

English Channel

Chicken		
Sheep		
Fish		
Pork		
Cattle		
Potatoes		
Sugar Beet		
Dairy		
Vegetables		
Grains		

Seine

Paris

FRANCE

Atlantic Ocean

Hebrides

The United Kingdom

The British Isles is a group of islands that includes the island of Great Britain, which is made up of three countries—England, Wales, and Scotland— and the island of Ireland, which consists of Ireland and the Republic of Northern Ireland. Long ago, these nations often fought with each other. In the 12th century, England conquered Wales. It united with Scotland in the 18th century. The three nations became known as the United Kingdom of Great Britain, or the UK.

Ireland became part of the United Kingdom in 1801 but separated from the UK in 1921. The Republic of Northern Ireland separated from Ireland and remains part of the United Kingdom.

The four nations are independent countries that share one monarch, Queen Elizabeth II, and a parliament or legislature, which passes laws for the United Kingdom as a whole. The capital of the United Kingdom is London, England.

dairy products, and fresh garden vegetables are among their favorites.

Beef, Lamb, and Pork

The English are meat eaters. When migrating tribes from the European continent first settled in England in 4000 B.C., they found wild sheep, cattle, and pigs already on the island. Domesticating and raising the animals for food has been a part of English rural life ever since. Up until the 18th century, English cattle were small and

Black pudding, which is made from pig's blood, oatmeal, and onions, is one of several types of sausages enjoyed in England.

their meat was tough. English farmers experimented with cattle breeding, which produced larger animals with more tender meat. Today, breeding livestock is a major English industry.

Other than during World War II when meat was **rationed** in order to ensure there was enough to feed the military troops, meat has usually been plentiful in England. It is not uncommon for people to eat meat at least once a day. Meat is roasted, ground, boiled with carrots and dumplings, fried, added to soups, covered with sauce, and turned into sausages and savory puddings and pies

And, very little is wasted. According to chef and television host Anthony Bourdain, the English use everything from "nose to tail."[1] For instance, calf's kidneys are baked into pies and ox tails are cooked in stew. **Suet** (SOO-it), the fat from around a sheep or cow's kidneys, is used to make dumplings and sweet puddings.

Pig's blood is the main ingredient in black pudding, a type of sausage. To make it, pig's blood is mixed with onions and oatmeal and poured into a casing made from a pig's intestines. Other varieties of sausages or **bangers,** as they are also called in England, feature beef or pork. They are eaten for breakfast, lunch, and supper, and are very popular. Marie Rayner, a food blogger who lives in England, explains: "We love our sausages …. They are rather meaty for one thing. Not small by any stretch …. You just can't beat a good British sausage."[2]

Fine Dairy Products

England is famous for its dairy products, especially its cheeses and cream. The English have been making a wide variety of cheese since at least the 11th century. Cheshire, cheddar, and Stilton cheeses are among the most famous. They are each named for the English county where they were first made. Cheshire may be the oldest of all English cheeses. It is a semi-hard cheese with a crumbly texture and a slightly salty taste that the English love.

Stilton and cheddar are other favorites. In fact, Stilton is often called the king of English cheeses. It is a soft, blue-veined cheese with a strong aroma. Cheese makers add harmless bacteria to the cheese as it ages, which causes its blue veins and its sharp odor and flavor.

Cheddar is probably the best known of all English cheeses. This golden-orange cheese is produced in wheels that weigh about 65 pounds (29.48kg) each. The cheese has a tangy, nutty taste. It is the main ingredient in a ploughman's lunch. This traditional meal that farmers ate as they worked consists of a chunk of cheese, a piece of bread, and pickled onions. Cheddar, as well as other cheeses, is also used in cooking and baking. And, cheese is traditionally served after dessert as a way to end a meal.

English clotted cream, too, is famous. This thick, mildly sweet cream is often served with pastries and tea. To make clotted cream, milk is heated then cooled

A ploughman's lunch is made up of food that farmers could easily take with them into the fields to eat, including cheese, pickled onions, and bread.

slowly. As the milk cools, the cream rises to the top and forms into thick clumps, or clots. Clotted cream is often compared to whipped cream. However, according to the authors of British Food, a website all about English cooking, "With its rich flavor and creamy thickness … many think this comparison gives clotted cream little justice."[3]

Cheese Toasties

Cheese toasties are popular in England. They make a light lunch, snack, or party treat. They are very easy to make. The toasties can be heated in a broiler, toaster oven, microwave oven, or baked in a full-size oven at 350°F. One slice of cooked bacon or fresh tomato can be placed on top of the toasties before heating, if desired.

Ingredients
1 cup shredded cheddar cheese
4 slices lightly toasted white or wheat bread
1 tablespoon mayonnaise
½ teaspoon grainy mustard
1 teaspoon milk
salt and pepper to taste

Instructions
1. Mix the cheese, mayonnaise, milk, chopped onions, mustard, salt and pepper together in a bowl.
2. Spread the cheese mixture on the toast.
3. Spray a baking sheet with nonstick cooking spray. Put the bread on the sheet. Toast until the cheese melts.
Serves 4.

About England

England occupies the southern two-thirds of the British Isles. It is the largest country in Great Britain, and is part of the United Kingdom, or the UK.

England is only 22 miles (35km) from France. It is separated from France by the English Channel. A tunnel called the Chunnel links England to the European continent.

England is a prosperous nation of about 50 million people. English is the national language. Football, which is the same as American soccer, is the most popular sport.

Throughout history, England has influenced world culture. The Magna Carta, an English document that was written in 1215, limited the power of government. It gave people rights and liberties and became a model for democracies throughout the world.

The influence of English artists such as poet and playwright William Shakespeare, Harry Potter creator J.K. Rowling, and the musical group the Beatles has also been widespread.

Fish and Seafood

Fish and seafood are also key ingredients in the English people's diet. England has 2,017 miles (3,246 km) of coastline. In the past, fish and seafood were so plentiful that they sold for pennies per pound. It was a common sight to see peddlers pushing wheelbarrows piled with oysters through the streets of London. In the 20th century, **overfishing** decreased the fish population and raised the price of fish. The English government was

Kippers and herring, traditional breakfast foods in England, are smoked over a fire.

Foods of England

quick to react. It passed laws to protect the fish population. Today fish and seafood are once again abundant.

On average, the English eat about 45 pounds (20.41kg) of fish and seafood per person per year. In comparison, Americans eat an annual average of 16 pounds (7.26kg) per person. Dover sole, cod, herring, and haddock are just a few of the fish the English enjoy.

Smoked herring and kippers are traditional breakfast foods. Before the invention of refrigeration, the English **smoked** fish to preserve it. They learned how to do so from the **Vikings**, who settled in England in the 9th century.

First the fish is coated with a salt mixture, which helps preserve it. Then it is hung in a smoky room. The smoke gives the fish an earthy flavor and aroma. Today, smoking fish to preserve it is no longer necessary. The English still do so, however, because they like the taste of smoked fish.

Fresh from English Gardens

The English also like the flavor of fresh vegetables, which many people grow in their own **kitchen gardens**. England's climate is ideal for gardening. Almost everyone who has a place to plant a garden does so. Many gardeners have separate flower and kitchen gardens. A kitchen garden is a small vegetable-and-herb patch located close to the kitchen, which makes it easy for cooks to run out and pluck fresh produce at any

Strawberries and Cream

Many people in England grow strawberries in their gardens. Fresh strawberries are plentiful in England in June and July. Strawberries and cream is a popular treat.

Ingredients
1 cup sour cream or plain Greek yogurt
½ cup sugar
1 pint strawberries

Instructions
1. Wash the strawberries. Remove the green tops. Cut the strawberries into quarters. Put them in a large bowl.
2. Mix the sour cream and sugar well.
3. Add the sour cream to the strawberries. Stir well.
4. Chill for one hour before serving.

Serves 4.

Strawberries and cream are a traditional English treat.

time. Peas, carrots, mint, and potatoes are some of the foods commonly grown in kitchen gardens.

Whether picked from a kitchen garden or purchased in a store, fresh locally grown vegetables are popular

A man harvests potatoes from his kitchen garden. English cooks often grow small crops of vegetables and herbs at home so they can use fresh ingredients in their meals.

ingredients in English cooking. In fact, a meal is not considered complete unless it contains meat or fish plus two vegetables, one of which is almost always potatoes. New, or baby, vegetables are particularly popular. These vegetables are picked when they are still small, which makes them sweeter and more tender than older, larger vegetables. English chef and author Jane Garmey says that when it comes to vegetables, in this case peas, "If you cannot get new, small peas, it's not worth buying those dreadful large bullets that appear every summer in most supermarkets."[4]

Boiled new potatoes, baby carrots cooked in butter and sugar, and young peas cooked with mint are just a few local favorites. The English prefer cooked vegetables to raw. This preference may stem from an ancient English notion that eating raw vegetables caused illness.

Vegetables are also cooked into pies and puddings, and they are turned into sauces. Horseradish sauce, for instance, is a popular topping with roast beef. And potatoes, in particular, are used in anything and everything.

English cooks have lots of other ingredients to add to their cooking. England's climate, location, and rich soil provide its people with multiple food choices. Yet, no matter what other foods they select, English cooks cannot do without local meat, dairy products, seafood, and vegetables. These foods are an important part of English life.

chapter 2

Simple and Delicious

The English people's favorite dishes are simple, filling, and delicious. Roast beef with Yorkshire pudding, savory pies, fish-and-chips, and fried breakfasts are especially popular.

Sunday Roast

The English have been eating roasted meat on Sunday for centuries. In the **Middle Ages**, it was common for wealthy landowners to roast an ox for their workers, or **serfs,** on Sunday. This practice evolved into a Sunday ritual in which English families get together over a large midday meal featuring roasted lamb, pork, or beef; with roast beef being the national favorite. The meal,

The traditional Sunday meal in England, which includes roast beef, vegetables, pudding, and gravy, has its origins in the Middle Ages.

according to English writer Elaine Lemm, "is the very heart of British food and cooking."[5]

Preparing the meal, which typically includes meat, a savory pudding, gravy, potatoes, peas and carrots, and horseradish sauce, takes time and energy. Usually enough food is made so that there are leftovers. Before the invention of the washing machine, having leftovers on Monday was especially important. Monday was the traditional laundry day, which was an all-day event that left little time for cooking. Having leftover meat that could be served cold or reheated for supper on Monday helped English housewives considerably.

Yorkshire Pudding

Yorkshire pudding almost always accompanies Sunday roast beef. The English make dozens of sweet or savory dishes that they call pudding. Yorkshire pudding falls

Horseradish Sauce

Horseradish sauce is easy to make. The English eat it with hot or cold roast beef. It is also a good accompaniment to fish.

Ingredients
3 tablespoons white horseradish, drained
1 teaspoon white wine vinegar
½ teaspoon sugar
½ teaspoon English (grainy) mustard
½ cup sour cream
1 teaspoon chopped chives

Instructions
Mix all the ingredients together. Chill for at least two hours before serving.
Makes about a ½ cup of sauce.

Horseradish sauce is typically served with roast beef and fish.

into the savory category. Made from a batter of flour, butter, eggs, and milk, Yorkshire pudding is similar to muffins or dumplings. It is baked in a pan or in a muffin tin coated with meat drippings. The meat drippings moisten and flavor the pudding, which puffs up and turns golden brown as it bakes.

Yorkshire pudding is served piping hot and smothered in gravy. It is soft, moist, and quite rich. In fact, in the past it was often served before the meal as a hearty appetizer. Diners filled up on the pudding and ate less meat. This ensured there would be plenty of leftovers for washday.

Yorkshire pudding, served hot and covered in gravy, is usually enjoyed alongside roast beef during a Sunday meal in England.

Interesting Names

Many English foods have interesting names. Toad in the hole is a good example. It is a savory pudding like Yorkshire pudding filled with sausage. Bubble and squeak is a fried dish made of cabbage and mashed potatoes. It gets its name from the sound the ingredients make while they are cooking. It is often topped with wow-wow sauce, a spicy sauce made with butter, mustard, and vinegar.

Angels on horseback is another dish with an interesting name. It consists of oysters wrapped in bacon and served on toast. Scotch woodcock is a version of scrambled eggs. And, cockie leekie is a hearty chicken and leek soup. Leeks are similar to onions.

Many desserts also have odd names. Jam roly-poly is a sweet steamed pudding filled with strawberry jam. Spotted dog is another steamed pudding. Raisins give it spots. Flummery is a slippery custard made with cream, gelatin, and almonds.

Savory Pies

Just as the English enjoy savory puddings, they also enjoy savory pies. Meat, vegetables, and/or fish encased in pastry have been a mainstay of English cooking and a favorite meal for centuries.

The English first started making savory pies in the Middle Ages, the time period from 500 to 1500 A.D. and before the invention of refrigerators. Enclosing meat in dough kept air away from the meat, which kept it from spoiling. Pork pies, which cooks during the Middle Ages

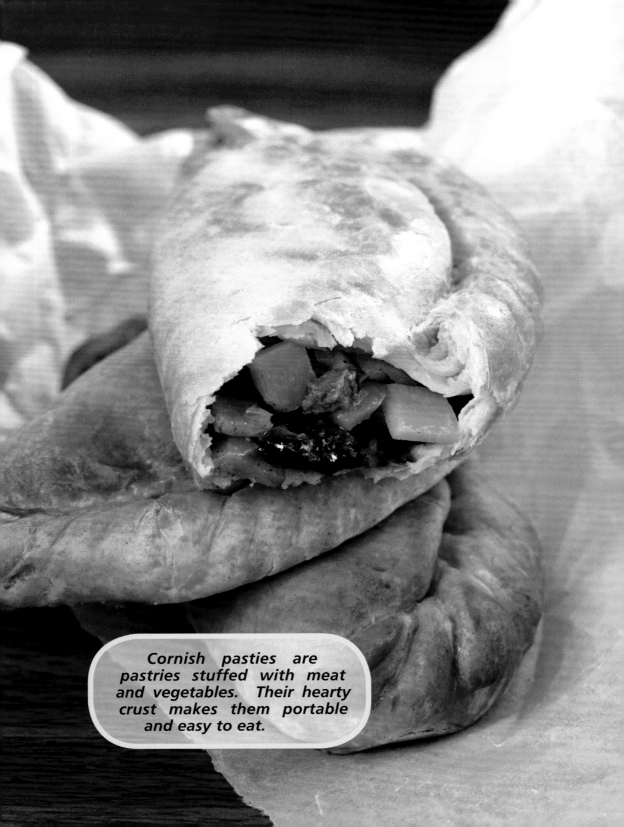

Cornish pasties are pastries stuffed with meat and vegetables. Their hearty crust makes them portable and easy to eat.

described as baked in a pastry coffin, and **mincemeat** pies, miniature pies filled with finely chopped lamb or beef, suet, chopped apples, and raisins, were early favorites. In fact, **Queen Elizabeth I**, who ruled from the mid to late 1500s, was reported to be a great fan of mincemeat pies.

The British make many varieties of savory pies in different sizes and shapes. Steak and kidney, chicken and mushroom, bacon and egg, and shepherd's pie, a lamb-and-vegetable pie topped with a mashed potato crust, are popular favorites. So are Cornish pasties (PASS-tees). They are fat semicircular pastry pouches that are traditionally filled with beef, potatoes, turnips, and onions. They originated in Cornwall, a region in England that was known for its tin mines. Pasties were a perfect meal for the tin miners who ate lunch deep in the mines, where they were not able to wash their dirty hands before eating. They were, however, able to hold a pasty by the corners of its thick crust without contaminating most of the food. When they finished eating, they tossed the dirty corners on the ground for the knockers, elves that they believed lived in the mines.

Unlike modern pasties, the miners' pasties contained meat and vegetables on one end and fruit or jam on the other. This provided them with a two-course meal—a main course and dessert. And, unlike most savory pastries, the filling in Cornish pasties is not cooked before it is put inside the dough. Because the meat and vegetables are chopped small, there is little risk that the meat will be undercooked, which could lead to food poisoning. Instead, the end result is crisp on the outside and moist and steaming hot on the inside. Allen, a food blogger, describes Cornish pasties as "a delightful meat and vegetable pie …. Not only is the pasty a practical food, easily packed in a lunchbox, but

Slow Cooker Roast Beef

Here is an easy way to make roast beef using a slow cooker. Spices and vegetables can be added according to taste. Low fat/ low sodium soup can be used.

Ingredients
3-pound chuck roast
1 10 ¾-ounce can cream of mushroom soup
1 tablespoon dry onion soup mix
1 onion peeled and quartered
1 cup baby carrots
4 small potatoes washed well and quartered (no need to peel)
¼ cup water
1 teaspoon each thyme, garlic powder, pepper

Instructions
1. Put the vegetables on the bottom of a 4 ½ quart slow cooker.
2. Put the roast on top of the vegetables.
3. Mix together the cream of mushroom soup, onion soup mix, spices, and water. Pour over the roast and vegetables.
4. Cover the pot. Cook on low six to eight hours or until the meat is fork tender.
Serves 6.

it is filled with savory richness and is a delight to crack open."[6]

Fish-and-Chips

Fish-and-chips is another simple and delicious dish that the English people love. There are **"chippies,"** restaurants and take-away shops that specialize in fish-and-chips, all over England.

The first chippies opened up in London in the 19th century during the **industrial revolution**, a time in history when many people moved from the countryside into the cities to work in factories. Chippies provided city dwellers with a cheap hot meal that they could

A "chippie" on Brighton Pier in England sells traditional fish and chips to visitors, who can either enjoy their meals in the restaurant or take them to go. The English like to top their fish and chips with vinegar and salt.

grab after a long day's work. Railroads were built during the industrial revolution that connected port cities to the rest of England and made it possible to supply inland chippies with an abundance of fresh fish.

Modern chippies are busy places, especially on Friday, which is the traditional day for the English to eat fish-and-chips. The custom developed long ago when many English people did not eat meat on Friday for religious reasons. Over time, eating fish-and-chips for supper on Friday has become an English tradition.

The British Empire

From the 15th through the early 20th century, England, and later the United Kingdom, ruled over territories throughout the world. The British Empire was the largest empire the world has ever known. It ruled over 20 percent of the Earth's land and 23 percent of its population.

At some point, the British Empire controlled or occupied what is now the United States, Canada, parts of Central America, the Republic of Ireland, Uganda, Gambia, Kenya, Nigeria, Afghanistan, India, Pakistan, Malaysia, Burma, Hong Kong, Singapore, Australia, New Zealand, much of the Middle East, and numerous islands in the Caribbean Sea and the South Pacific.

Today almost all the territories ruled by the British Empire are independent nations. Fifty-four of these nations, along with the United Kingdom, formed an association known as the Commonwealth of Nations whose goal is to help each other.

At a chippie, customers place their order at a counter. The fish, which is typically a mild-tasting white fish like cod, sole, or plaice, is dipped in batter and deep fried in hot bubbling oil until it is crisp and golden. It is served with **chips**, the English name for fried potatoes or french fries. The chips are quite a bit wider than American fries. And, unlike in many American fast-food restaurants, the chips are never frozen. They are made fresh, which gives them a dense texture.

Once the fish-and-chips are fried to perfection, they are packed in a thick sheet of paper, which keeps them hot and moist. The English like to sprinkle vinegar and salt on top of the fish-and-chips. Mushy peas, which are peas cooked with sugar, mint, and salt until they are the consistency of paste, often accompany the meal. Customers may eat in the chippie, in picnic areas, or take the fish home. "We live by the sea," explain the authors of Hidden England, a website dedicated to all things English. "Sitting on the seawall with a bundle of paper in our laps containing fish-and-chips covered with salt and vinegar … can only be described as sheer heaven."[7]

Breakfast Lovers

A hearty breakfast, designed to fuel people for the day ahead, is another English speciality. Although menus vary, a typical English breakfast, which is also known as a fried breakfast, is likely to include eggs, bacon, grilled tomatoes, fried bread, and sweet milky tea. Oatmeal, kippers, and sausage are other breakfast favorites. In

A typical English breakfast includes eggs, bacon, tomatoes, and milky tea.

the past, all these foods plus black pudding, cold meat, baked beans, rolls, toast, marmalade, and fruit were likely to be served. Since modern people have less time for breakfast, the meal has become smaller, but it is still hearty. It is especially popular on the weekend, when people do not have to rush off to work or school.

Many English people say that the best part of the meal is the way the many flavors and textures complement each other. Gamey says, "A grilled tomato on its own is good, but served . . . with bacon and fried bread, it can become extraordinary."[8]

For centuries, dishes like grilled tomatoes with bacon, eggs, and fried bread, fish-and-chips, roast beef and Yorkshire pudding, and savory pies have provided the English people with wonderful meals. It is no wonder that these simple and delicious dishes are English favorites.

Chapter 3

It Is Time for Tea

Drinking tea is a way of life in England. Taking a tea break is the English people's favorite way to snack. The snack may be no more than a **"cuppa,"** a simple cup of tea. Or, it may be a large spread featuring pastries, little sandwiches, and clotted cream set up around a porcelain teapot. Either way, the English love tea. Afternoon tea is a beloved tradition in which people stop what they are doing to relax over a pot of tea with friends. According to novelist Henry James who lived in England for 30 years, "There are few hours in life more agreeable than the hour dedicated to the ceremony known as afternoon tea."[9]

The Indian Influence

The British ruled India for about 200 years. Many English people living in India hired Indian cooks. These Indian cooks adapted spicy Indian dishes to British tastes. Many of the dishes they created became popular in England. In fact, there are many Indian restaurants in England.

Mulligatawny (mull-ih-guh-TAW-nee) soup is one such dish. This creamy chicken soup is flavored with curry powder, a premade spice mix that features many of the spices used in India. Kedgeree, a popular breakfast dish, is another. It consists of smoked fish, onions, and hard-boiled eggs served on rice and topped with a spicy sauce. Chutney, a spicy condiment made with fruit, chili peppers, and multiple spices in India is also popular in England. However, English chutney is less spicy and more sweet and fruity.

A Long History

Per person, the English are the fifth-largest consumers of tea in the world, with each person drinking about six cups a day. They drink tea with meals, in between meals, at meetings, dances, and sporting events. Tea is always offered to guests, and tea parties are a charming English custom.

Dutch traders, who brought tea from Asia, introduced the beverage to the English in the 17th century. At that time, only the rich could afford it. It became cheaper and more plentiful in the 19th century, when England ruled over India and controlled that nation's

A sketch from the 1870s depicts a mother making tea in her home in the slums of London. Once consumed only by the rich, tea became inexpensive in England during the 19th century, which made drinking it a custom among the lower classes as well.

Royalty and Nobility

England is a constitutional monarchy. It is ruled by elected officials and by Queen Elizabeth II, but her power is limited. The queen is a member of the English royal family. Royalty and nobility are people who inherit titles, land, and privileges based on their family ties. The highest members of English nobility are the royal family. Kings, queens, princes, and princesses are part of a royal family.

English nobles are not part of the royal family. The nobles with the most authority are dukes and duchesses. Next are marquesses (MAR-kwiss-is) and marchionesses (MAR-shuh-ness-is). Earls and countesses, viscounts (VIE-counts) and viscountesses, and finally barons and baronesses follow them.

Knights are not members of the nobility. They are people who earn recognition from a king or queen for noteworthy achievements. In the Middle Ages, knights were warriors who served nobles in return for land or favors.

tea plantations. Soon, everyone in England was drinking tea.

An 18th-century English **duchess** who complained of feeling tired, hungry, and bored in the afternoon started the ritual of afternoon tea by inviting friends for tea and pastries. It was not long before other **noble** women took up the habit. When tea became less expensive more and more people were able to buy and enjoy tea. In fact, 19th-century English factory workers were given an afternoon tea break. The caffeine in the tea gave them energy to keep working into the evening.

Not Just Any Tea

Not just any tea will do. The English are particular about their tea. They prefer strong black tea from Asia. To make tea, English cooks fill a kettle with fresh water. They never reboil the water. Doing so, they say, ruins the taste of the tea. The kettle is heated until the water boils. The water is poured into a teapot along with one tea bag per person, plus one extra tea bag for the pot. The tea bag is left to steep, or soak in the hot water, for about five minutes. A special cover known as a tea cozy is put over the teapot to keep it warm. The tea is usually served with milk and sugar.

Scones and Cream

Scones, pastries similar to American biscuits, are a popular food eaten with tea. Scones originated in Scotland in the 16th century and quickly became popular in England. Early scones were made of oats and cooked on a griddle.

Modern scones are made with flour, baking soda, butter, eggs, sugar, and milk, and are baked in an oven. They often contain raisins. They are light and fluffy with a crisp crust and a hint of sweetness. The English eat them warm, topped with butter, strawberry jam, and, sometimes, fresh clotted cream.

When clotted cream is served with scones at afternoon tea, it is known as a cream tea. Cream teas are usually elegant affairs. Hosts use their finest china and

An elegant cream tea setting includes scones with jam and clotted cream served on fine china.

table linens. **Tea rooms**, restaurants, and hotels in England offer cream teas. English chef Miles Collins says, "A warm freshly baked fruit scone with a smear of homemade strawberry jam and dollop of thick Cornish [clotted] cream all washed down with a pot of tea [is] sheer … bliss. Great Britain on a plate."[10]

Assorted Pastries

In addition to scones, a variety of other pastries often accompanies afternoon tea. Cookies, which are known as biscuits in England, are especially popular. Favorites, according to New York chef Melissa Plotkin, include "plain and chocolate digestives, flat round cookies; Jammy Dodgers, cookies with strawberry jam, and custard creams, [and] vanilla cream cookies."[11]

Rock cakes are another favorite. Rock cakes look like lumpy raisin cookies. In fact, they got their name because of their rough bumpy appearance. Despite the way they look, rock cakes are soft and chewy and taste sweet.

Fat rascals, which taste a lot like rock cakes, are also popular biscuits or cookies. Fat rascals originated in the 16th century as a way for bakers to use leftover pastry dough. They were originally called turf cakes because they were cooked on a griddle over an open fire fueled by turf, or dried grass. Modern fat rascals are plump dome-shaped cookies filled with dried fruit. The cook-

A couple enjoys fat rascals and tea at Betty's, a famous bakery and tea room in England.

Victoria Sponge Cake

Here is an easy one-layer Victoria sponge cake.

Ingredients
1 cup flour
2 eggs
1 cup sugar
1 teaspoon vanilla
1 teaspoon baking soda
1 teaspoon baking powder
½ cup milk
1 tablespoon unsalted butter
¼ teaspoon of salt
⅓ cup whipped cream
¼ cup strawberry jam

Instructions
1. Preheat the oven to 350°F.
2. Beat the eggs well. Add the vanilla and sugar. Mix well.
3. Combine the flour, salt, and baking powder. Add to the egg mixture. Stir to form a batter.
4. Combine the milk and butter and microwave until the milk almost boils. Mix into the batter.
5. Spray an 8–9 inch (20.3cm–22.8cm) cake pan with nonstick cooking spray. Pour in the batter. Bake for about 30 minutes or until a fork placed in the middle of the cake comes out dry.
6. Let the cake cool for about 15 minutes. Put the cake on a plate. Spread the strawberry preserves and whipped cream on the top of the cake.

Makes one cake. Serves 8.

ies are decorated with two cherries to stand for eyes, and two almonds in the shape of a snarling mouth. The silly face makes the cookies a special favorite of English children. In fact, they are so popular that Betty's, an English bakery and tea room famous for these cookies, makes and sells about 350,000 a year.

A Queen's Favorite

Victoria sponge cake, too, is a popular accompaniment to tea. This soft, moist, and spongy cake is made up of two layers held together with strawberry jam and whipped cream, and topped with powdered sugar. It is named after **Queen Victoria** who ruled England during the 19th century. She loved the cake and served it at tea parties.

A baker sifts powdered sugar on top of a Victoria sponge cake, so named because it was a favorite treat of Queen Victoria.

Sponge cake can be tricky to make. Eggs give the cake its unique texture, but too many eggs can overwhelm the flavor. In the past, English bakers used a scale to help them figure out the right balance of ingredients. Author Marguerite Patten explains: "The classic method of gauging the amount was to place the eggs on scales and balance the fat, sugar, and flour against them."[12]

Tea Sandwiches

Making tea sandwiches requires less measuring and more creativity. The dainty little sandwiches often are eaten with tea and are also served for a light meal. The Earl of Sandwich, an 18th-century English nobleman, is believed to be the inventor of the modern sandwich. According to legend, he loved to play cards and often played through mealtimes. Instead of getting up to eat a formal meal, the earl had two pieces of bread stuffed with cold roast beef brought to him. Prepared this way, the food was easy to hold and eat while still playing cards. His invention, which was called a sandwich after the earl, soon became popular in England.

Tea sandwiches are smaller and thinner than those the earl ate. They are snack sandwiches that are made with thin, soft, white bread with no crusts. Tea sandwiches are almost always spread with a fine layer of butter, which keeps the bread from getting soggy, and they are made with a variety of fillings. Cookie cutters are used to cut the tea sandwiches into quarters, delicate long fingers, or decorative shapes.

Tuna Tea Sandwiches

These little sandwiches are easy to make. For fun, instead of cutting the sandwiches into squares with a knife, use cookie cutters to cut the sandwiches into interesting shapes.

Ingredients
6 slices white or wheat bread, crusts removed
1 4 ½-ounce can of tuna fish, drained well
1 tablespoon mayonnaise
½ teaspoon pepper
1 tablespoon butter
6 green leaf lettuce leaves

Instructions
1. Spread each slice of bread with a thin layer of butter.
2. Combine the tuna fish, mayonnaise, and pepper in a bowl. Mix well, breaking up any large chunks of tuna.
3. Spread a thin layer of tuna on three slices of bread. Top with a lettuce leaf and another slice of bread.
4. Cut each sandwich into quarters.
Makes 12 tea sandwiches.

Tea sandwiches made with tuna or other ingredients are often served as a light meal in England.

The fillings can be anything that is light and easy to digest. A typical sandwich might contain cream cheese and paper-thin slices of cucumber; a leaf of watercress (a peppery, green water plant) sprinkled with salt; tuna salad; or a slice of turkey with raspberry jam. Peanut butter and banana sandwiches are a favorite at children's tea parties.

The light fresh taste of tea sandwiches enhances the flavor of tea. So too does the taste of flaky scones, light-as-air sponge cake, fruit-filled cookies, and of course, the company of friends. Together they make afternoon tea a special part of the English people's day, and a very pleasant tradition.

Chapter 4

Happy Holidays

The English celebrate holidays with special foods traditionally associated with the occasion. Christmas goose, Christmas pudding, pancakes, hot cross buns, and Easter eggs are among these special foods.

Merry Christmas

Christmas is a festive time in England. Christmas dinner, which is eaten in the middle of the afternoon on Christmas day, is a huge feast. Menus vary, but it is likely that roast goose or turkey will be the main course. Roast goose is the more traditional dish. Up until the mid-20th century, when turkey became popular, roast goose was almost always the centerpiece of Christmas gatherings. In fact, in the classic 19th-century English

A roasted goose topped with strips of bacon and filled with savory stuffing is a traditional Christmas meal in England.

novel, *A Christmas Carol* by **Charles Dickens**, roast goose is served for Christmas dinner.

Goose is moist and has a rich flavor similar to beef. An extra layer of fat under the bird's skin drips onto the meat as it cooks, keeping moisture in. Goose is prepared much like a turkey. Its skin is usually rubbed with butter and sprinkled with salt, pepper, and a savory spice called sage. Sometimes it is covered with slices of bacon. The inside of the bird is filled with stuffing. Fried onions and sage; apples and prunes; or apples, sausage, and sage are all common types of stuffing. Potatoes, cranberries, brussels sprouts, and plenty of rich gravy are popular accompaniments.

Suzanna Austin, an English woman, describes her family's holiday meal: "At Christmas dinner … there are two roasted meats one being either goose or turkey covered in bacon and stuffed with sausage meat, the other meat being a gammon [ham]. [There are a] variety of seasonal vegetables but essential are roast potatoes and brussel[s] sprouts and always kilted sausage [sausage wrapped in pastry]."[13]

An English Tradition

Christmas dinner is not complete without Christmas pudding for dessert. Serving it on Christmas has been an English tradition since the 18th century.

Making the pudding takes time. Traditionally, it is cooked four Sundays before Christmas on "stir-up Sunday." The day gets its name because it is the custom for every family member to stir the pudding as it

Boxing Day

Boxing Day is an English holiday that is celebrated on December 26th, the day after Christmas. Traditionally, gifts are given to the poor on Boxing Day. In the past English families kept a clay container with a slit on the top in their homes. The container was known as the Christmas box. Families put spare change in it throughout the year. The box was opened on Boxing Day and its contents were given to the needy. Churches kept alms boxes, which served the same purpose.

English people still give donations to charity on Boxing Day. They also give monetary tips to household help, mail carriers, and delivery people. Mounted fox hunts, horse races, and English football (soccer) matches are held on Boxing Day. Many families get together for a meal of Christmas leftovers on Boxing Day.

Christmas pudding, which takes several weeks to make, is usually covered with brandy and lit in order to be brought to the table topped with a flame.

cooks while making a Christmas wish.

The pudding is made with dried fruits, spices, bread-crumbs, dark brown sugar, suet, fruit juice or dark beer, and black **treacle**, a sweet, dark syrup. The mixture is poured into a tightly covered mold, which is placed in a pot of boiling water and steamed over low heat for three to seven hours.

When the pudding is done, it is wrapped in foil and stored in a cool, dark place until Christmas day. During this time, the different flavors and scents blend together and become stronger. Before the pudding is served, it is steamed again. Brandy, an alcoholic beverage, is often poured over the top and set afire. The lights are dimmed and the flaming pudding is brought to the table. According to chef Melissa Plotkin, "It tastes more like cake than pudding. It is very moist and springy.

Spiced Cranberries

Cranberries are often served with Christmas dinner. This is a simple, tasty side dish. Pineapples can be added if desired. Walnuts can be substituted for pecans.

Ingredients
1 16-ounce can whole cranberries
1 navel orange
⅓ cup raisins
¼ cup chopped pecans
1 ½ teaspoons cinnamon
1 teaspoon ground ginger

Instructions
1. Put the cranberries in a bowl.
2. Peel and section the orange. Cut the sections into small pieces.
3. Add the orange pieces, raisins, nuts, ginger, and cinnamon to the cranberries. Mix well.
4. Cover and refrigerate for at least 30 minutes.
Serves 4–6.

It is traditionally served with brandy butter—butter, brandy and sugar, or whipped cream."[14]

Pancake Tuesday

Pancakes are another time-honored English holiday food. Customarily, the English eat, toss, and take part in pancake races on Shrove Tuesday, the day before Lent. Lent is the 40-day period leading up to Easter. For religious reasons, many people give up eating sweets,

Women holding frying pans take part in a pancake race, a traditional event held on Shrove Tuesday in many English towns.

often made with eggs, sugar, and butter, during this time. Pancake Tuesday started in the Middle Ages as a way for Christians who observed Lent to use up these foods before Lent began. Today, most English people celebrate Pancake Tuesday whether or not they are Christians.

English cooks make pancakes in a frying pan and flip them into the air. On Pancake Tuesday, towns throughout England hold pancake races. The object of these races is to reach the finish line first while flipping a pancake in a frying pan a set number of times. The pancake must be in one piece at the end in order for the contestant to win. According to English legend, the idea for pancake races comes from a housewife in the 15th century, who, thinking she was late for Shrove Tuesday services, ran to church holding a hot frying pan and tossing pancakes into the air.

Unlike thick, fluffy American pancakes, English pancakes are light and paper thin. They are topped with butter, sugar, and a splash of lemon juice. The pancakes are rolled up into cylinders and eaten while they are piping hot.

Hot Cross Buns

Easter arrives with other traditional foods such as hot cross buns. These sweet, filled buns are eaten on Good Friday, two days before Easter. The buns are decorated with a cross on top. It represents the cross on which Christians believe Jesus Christ was put to death.

The English have been eating hot cross buns for centuries. Food historians believe they were eaten in ancient times to celebrate the arrival of spring. At that time, the cross on top probably symbolized the four phases of the moon.

In the 18th and 19th centuries, street vendors all over England sold the buns for a penny apiece. Their cries have since become the words of a children's nursery rhyme. Back then the cross was cut into the dough, and the filling was made of cinnamon and raisins. And, because the buns had a cross on top, they were

Hot cross buns, so named because of their cross-shaped decoration, are served in England on Good Friday.

believed to have healing powers. In fact, many people hung a bun in their kitchen to protect their family from disease. Today the buns are sold in supermarkets. The cross is made with icing, and the filling can be almost anything.

Despite these differences, the buns still remain a symbol of Easter in England. According to English journalist Tessa Cunningham, "Hot cross buns are as much a part of Easter as daffodils and chocolate eggs. … [They are] as quintessentially [typically] British as roast beef and Yorkshire pudding."[15]

Easter Eggs

Easter eggs, too, are a part of English Easter celebrations. Eggs have long been a symbol of Easter and spring. The English have been decorating, hiding, hunting for, rolling, and eating eggs on Easter since the Middle Ages. In fact, the idea of the Easter Bunny is probably based on an ancient English legend about a rabbit that laid eggs.

Early English Easter eggs were bird's rather than chicken's eggs. They were dyed with fruit or vegetable juices, or with onionskin, which was tightly wrapped around the eggs before they were hardboiled. When the onionskins were removed, the eggs were colored a marbled brown, yellow, or red, depending on the shade of the onionskin used. Leaves and flowers were also placed on the eggshells to create even more intricate designs. In 1290 English king Edward I used thin sheets

English Pubs

For centuries, English pubs have been gathering places where people go to visit, drink beer, have a bite to eat, watch sporting events, and play pool or darts. Every English town has at least one pub.

Many English pubs are very old. The earliest pubs were known as alehouses or taverns. They were a place for travelers to stable their horses, eat, and stay for the night.

Some pubs are quite fancy inside, while others are plain. All have some sort of food available. Offerings range from snacks like bags of fried pork rinds to hot meals. There is usually a menu on the bar or posted on a chalkboard. Some pubs are child friendly. Many families go to these pubs to eat. In fact, some pubs have separate dining rooms and offer booster seats for young children. Many pubs also allow dogs.

of real gold to decorate 450 Easter eggs, which he gave out as gifts.

Modern English people usually decorate Easter eggs with store-bought dyes. And, since the 20th century

Easter Nests

Easter nests are fun to make. Crisp rice cereal, cornflakes, shredded wheat, or crisp chow mein noodles can be used for the nests. The chocolate can be milk chocolate, dark chocolate, or a combination of the two.

Ingredients
12 ounces chocolate chips
2 cups crushed corn flakes
½ cup shredded coconut flakes
Assorted jellybeans, miniature candy eggs, and/or marshmallow chicks

Instructions
1. Cover a baking sheet with wax paper or nonstick foil. Spray the foil or paper with nonstick cooking spray.
2. Put cornflakes and coconut in a bowl.
3. Put the chocolate in a microwave safe bowl. Microwave until the chocolate melts; about two to three minutes. Pour the chocolate over the cornflake mixture and stir until the mixture is covered with chocolate.
4. Spoon the chocolate mix onto the baking sheet, making ten to twelve mounds. Shape the mounds into round nests. Use a spoon to make a dent in the center of each round.
5. Refrigerate for at least one hour so the nests can harden. Put jellybeans, miniature candy eggs, and/or marshmallow chick in each nest.

Makes 10 to 12 nests.

A nest of shredded wheat holds two candy Easter eggs.

chocolate Easter eggs have become a national favorite. Over 80 million are sold each year. The eggs may be solid or filled with cream. They may be as large as an ostrich egg or as tiny as a hummingbird's. Miniature chocolate eggs sitting in little nests made of chocolate-covered dried cereal are a popular Easter treat.

Hunting for hidden Easter eggs and egg rolling add to the fun. Egg rolling is a centuries-old English custom in which colored eggs are rolled down a hill. Indeed, traditional foods and customs help make English holidays all the more memorable.

Metric conversions

Mass (weight)

1 ounce (oz.)	= 28.0 grams (g)
8 ounces	= 227.0 grams
1 pound (lb.) or 16 ounces	= 0.45 kilograms (kg)
2.2 pounds	= 1.0 kilogram

Liquid Volume

1 teaspoon (tsp.)	= 5.0 milliliters (ml)
1 tablespoon (tbsp.)	= 15.0 milliliters
1 fluid ounce (oz.)	= 30.0 milliliters
1 cup (c.)	= 240 milliliters
1 pint (pt.)	= 480 milliliters
1 quart (qt.)	= 0.96 liters (l)
1 gallon (gal.)	= 3.84 liters

Pan Sizes

8- inch cake pan	= 20 x 4-centimeter cake pan
9-inch cake pan	= 23 x 3.5-centimeter cake pan
11 x 7-inch baking pan	= 28 x 18-centimeter baking pan
13 x 9-inch baking pan	= 32.5 x 23-centimeter baking pan
9 x 5-inch loaf pan	= 23 x 13-centimeter loaf pan
2-quart casserole	= 2-liter casserole

Temperature

212°F	= 100°C (boiling point of water)
225°F	= 110°C
250°F	= 120°C
275°F	= 135°C
300°F	= 150°C
325°F	= 160°C
350°F	= 180°C
375°F	= 190°C
400°F	= 200°C

Length

1/4 inch (in.)	= 0.6 centimeters (cm)
1/2 inch	= 1.25 centimeters
1 inch	= 2.5 centimeters

Notes

Chapter 1: A Fertile Land

1. Anthony Bourdain: *No Reservations: London; Edinburgh*, February 2008, The Travel Channel, Christopher Collins, executive producer.

2. Marie Rayner. "Sweet and Sour Meatballs." The English Kitchen, November 3, 2009. http://theenglishkitchen.blogspot.com/2009/11/sweet-and-sour-meat-balls.html.

3. "Clotted Cream," British Food. www.britsfood.com/index.php?option=com_content&view=article&id=59&Itemid=69.

4. Jane Garmey. *Great British Cooking A Well Kept Secret*. New York: Harper Collins, 1992, p. 112.

Chapter 2: Simple and Delicious

5. Elaine Lemm. "Great British Sunday Lunch—The Sunday Roast." About.com, British Food. http://britishfood.about.com/od/introtobritishfood/tp/sundaylunch.htm.

6. Allen Williams. "English Pasty Recipe." Eating Out Loud, April 11, 2007. www.eatingoutloud.com/2007/04/english-food-is-not-a-joke-my-pasty-is-proof.html.

7. Traditional English Recipes Fish-and-Chips, Hidden England. http://hidden-england.netfirms.com/fishandchips.htm.

8. Jane Garmey. *Great British Cooking A Well Kept Secret*. p. 3.

Chapter 3: It Is Tea Time

9. "Henry James Quotes," Think Exist.com. http://thinkexist.com/quotation/there_are_few_hours_in_life_more_agreeable_than/171721.html.

10. Miles Collins. "How to Pronounce Scone." *Beyond the Kitchen*, May 19, 2010. www.milescollins.com/wordpress/how-to-pronounce-scone.

11. Melissa Plotkin. E-mail interview with the author, January 31, 2011.

12. Maguerite Patten. *Maguerite Patten's Century of British Cooking*. London: Grub Street, 1999, p. 36.

Chapter 4: Happy Holidays

13. Quoted in "Christmas in England, Santa's Net. www.santas.net /englishchristmas.htm.

14. Melissa Plotkin. E-mail interview with the author.

15. Tessa Cunningham. "How to … Bake Authentic Hot Cross Buns." *Mail Online*, March 29, 2010. www.dailymail.co.uk/femail/article-1261487/HOW-TO-bake-hot-cross-buns.html.

Glossary

bangers: English term for sausages.

Charles Dickens: Famous 19th-century English author.

chippies: Informal eateries that make and sell fish-and-chips.

chips: English term for french fries.

cuppa: English term for a cup of tea.

duchess: An English noblewoman who is married to a duke.

industrial revolution: Time in history when the factory system developed.

kitchen gardens: Small vegetable-and-herb gardens located near a home's kitchen.

Middle Ages: Time in history between the 5th and 15th centuries.

mincemeat: Finely chopped meat.

noble: Person of high birth who inherits a title, land, and privileges due to family ties.

overfishing: To exhaust the supply of available fish by catching too many.

Queen Elizabeth I: English queen who ruled from 1558–1603 and helped make England a world power.

Queen Victoria: English queen who ruled from 1838–1903. During her rule the British Empire expanded.

rationing: Limiting the amount of food or supplies allotted to people.

scones: Muffin-like pastries.

serfs: Farmworkers in the service of a nobleman or lord.

smoked: To preserve meat or fish by exposing it to smoke.

suet: Animal fat.

tea room: A shop where tea and accompaniments like pastries are served.

treacle: A sweet, dark syrup similar to corn syrup.

Vikings: Scandinavian sailors and pirates who raided England and the coast of Europe from the 8th to the 11th centuries.

Books

Alan Allport, George Wingfield. *England*. New York: Chelsea House, 2007. Looks at England's geography, government, history, and daily life.

Patrick Dillon. *The Story of Britain from the Norman Conquest to the European Union*. Somerset, MA: Candlewick, 2011. Examines the history of Great Britain from ancient times to the present.

Gavin Mortimer. *Find Out About the United Kingdom*. Hauppaugue, NY: Barron's Educational Series, 2009. Facts on the four countries that make up the United Kingdom, including a look at the lives of children living there.

Claire Throp. *England*. Chicago: Heinemann, 2011. Information about English life, culture, history, economics, and geography.

Websites

Food in Every Country: United Kingdom (www .foodbycountry.com/Spain-to-Zimbabwe-Cumulative-Index/United-Kingdom.html). This website explains the history of food in the United Kingdom; with recipes.

Project Britain (http://projectbritain.com/). This website is created by English school students. It has all sorts of information and pictures about British life and culture including information on food.

National Geographic for Kids: United Kingdom (http://kids.nationalgeographic.com/kids/places /find/united-kingdom/). A colorful website with lots of pictures, facts, a video, map, and e-cards.

Time for Kids: England (www.timeforkids.com /TFK/kids/hh/goplaces/article/0,28376,605516,00 .html). Provides facts, color photos, a map, video, and e-card.

Index

A

angels on horseback, 21

B

bacteria, added to cheese, 8
bangers. *See* sausages
beef
　Cornish pasties, *22*, 23–25
　history, 6–7
　horseradish sauce for, 16, 19
　roast beef recipe, 24
　Sunday roast, 17–19, *18*
　uses, 7–8
biscuits, 34–35, *35*, 37
black pudding, *7*, 8
Bourdain, Anthony, 7–8
Boxing Day, 43
breakfast, 27–28, *28*, 30
British Empire
　history, 26
　United Kingdom, 4, 6
bubble and squeak, 21

C

cake, sponge, 36, *37*, 37–38
charity donations, 43
cheddar cheese, 9
cheese toasties recipe, 10
cheeses, types, 8–9, *9*

Cheshire cheese, 8
chippies, *25*, 25–26
Christmas
　pudding, 43–45, *44*
　roast goose, 41–42, *42*
A Christmas Carol (Dickens),
　42
Chunnel, 11
chutney, 30
clotted cream, 9–10, 33–34, *34*
cockie leekie, 21
Commonwealth of Nations, 26
cookies, 34–35, *35*, 37
Cornish pasties, *22*, 23–25
cranberries recipe, 45
cream, clotted, 9–10, 33–34, *34*
cuppa, 29

D

dairy products
　clotted cream, 9–10, 33–34,
　34
　strawberries and cream rec-
　ipe, 14
desserts
　cheese, 9
　Christmas pudding, 43–45, *44*
　oddly named, 21
Dickens, Charles, 42

E
Earl of Sandwich, 38
Easter
  eggs, 48–51, *51*
  hot cross buns, 47–48, *48*
Easter nests recipe, 50
Elizabeth I, 23
Elizabeth II, 6, 32
England
  basic facts, 4, 11
  royalty and nobility, 6, 23, 32,
  38–40
English Channel, 11

F
fat rascals, *35*, 35, 37
fish, 11, 13
fish-and-chips, *25*, 25–27
flummery, 21
food names, 21
food regions map, 5
Friday supper, 26

G
gammon, 43
goose, 41–42, *42*
Great Britain, 4, 6

H
herring, smoked, *12*, 13
holiday foods
  Christmas pudding, 43–45, *44*
  Easter eggs, 48–51, *51*
  hot cross buns, 47–48, *48*
  pancakes, 45–47, *46*
  roast goose, 41–42, *42*

horseradish sauce, 16, 19

I
India, 30
industrial revolution, 25, 26

J
jam roly-poly, 21
James, Henry, 29

K
kedgeree, 30
king of English cheeses, 8
kippers, *12*, 13
kitchen gardens, 13–14, *15*
knights, 32
knockers, 23

L
leftovers, importance of, 18
Lent, 45
livestock, history, 6–7

M
Magna Carta, 11
meals
  breakfast, 27–28, *28*, 30
  Christmas dinner, 41–45, *42*,
  44
  Friday supper, 26
  miner's, *22*, 23–25
  Sunday midday, 17–20, *18*,
  20, 24
  traditional farmer's, 9
  typical, 15
  See also tea

meat
  Christmas dinner, 41–43, *42*
  history, 6–7, 21, 23
  importance, 7
  Sunday midday meal, 17–19,
  18, 24
mincemeat pies, 23
miners' meals, *22,* 23–25
mulligatawny soup, 30
mushy peas, 27

N
nobility, 32, 38–40

O
overfishing, 11, 13

P
Pancake Tuesday, 45–47, *46*
pasties, *22,* 23–25
pastries, 33–35, *34,* 37
peas, 14, 27
pies, 21, *22,* 23–25
population, 11
potatoes, *15,* 16
pubs, 49
puddings
  black, *7,* 8
  Christmas, 43–45, *44*
  savory, 19–20, *20,* 21

R
recipes
  cheese toasties, 10
  Easter nests, 50

horseradish sauce, 19
  slow cooker roast beef, 24
  spiced cranberries, 45
  strawberries and cream, 14
  tuna tea sandwiches, 39
  Victoria sponge cake, 36
roast beef, 17–19, *18,* 24
roast goose, 41–42, *42*
rock cakes, 35
royalty, 6, 23, 32

S
sandwiches for tea, 38–40
sausages
  black pudding, *7,* 8
  types, 8
  Yorkshire pudding, 19–20, *20,*
  21
savory pies, 21, *22,* 23–25
savory puddings, 19–20, *20,* 21
scones, 33–34
Scotch woodcock, 21
seafood, 11, 13
shepherd's pies, 23
Shrove Tuesday, 45
slow cooker roast beef recipe,
  24
snacks, cheese toasties, 10
soup, 30
spiced cranberries recipe, 45
spicy foods, 21, 30
sponge cake, 36, *37,* 37–38
spotted dog, 21
Stilton cheese, 8
stir-up Sunday, 43–44

strawberries and cream recipe, 14
suet, uses, 8
Sunday midday meals
  history, 17
  roast beef, 17–19, *18*, 24
  Yorkshire pudding, 19–20, *20*

T
tea
  afternoon, 29
  biscuits, 34–35, *35*, 37
  consumption, 30
  cream, 33–34, *34*
  history, 30, *31*, 32–33
  making, 33
  sandwiches, 38–40
  Victoria sponge cake, 36, *37*, 37–38
toad in the hole, 21
treacle, 44
tuna tea sandwiches recipe, 39
turf cakes, *35*, 35, 37

U
United Kingdom of Great Britain and Northern Ireland (UK), 4, 6

V
vegetables, 15–16
  cockie leekie, 21
  Cornish pasties, *22*, 23–25
  harvesting, *15*
  kitchen gardens, 13–14, *15*
  mushy peas, 27
Victoria sponge cake, 36, *37*, 37–38
Vikings, 13

W
wow-wow sauce, 21

Y
Yorkshire pudding, 19–20, *20*

Picture Credits

About the Author

Barbara Sheen is the author of more than 60 books for young people. She lives in New Mexico with her family. In her spare time, she likes to swim, walk, garden, and read. Of course, she loves to cook!